Dads Need Hugs Too

Children's Family Life Books

Speedy Publishing LLC
40 E. Main St. #1156
Newark, DE 19711
www.speedypublishing.com

Copyright 2016

All Rights reserved. No part of this book may be reproduced or used in any way or form or by any means whether electronic or mechanical, this means that you cannot record or photocopy any material ideas or tips that are provided in this book

Expressing love and care for your dad

Kids, in this book you will be learn the importance of hugging your dad. What is the essence of the act? Read on and feel its importance. Your dad needs to be hugged, too!

A father has a great positive impact on the lives of his children.

Being a father is not an easy stroll in the park. Although being a mother is equally tough, being a father takes thought and effort. He needs to be a great father for his children.

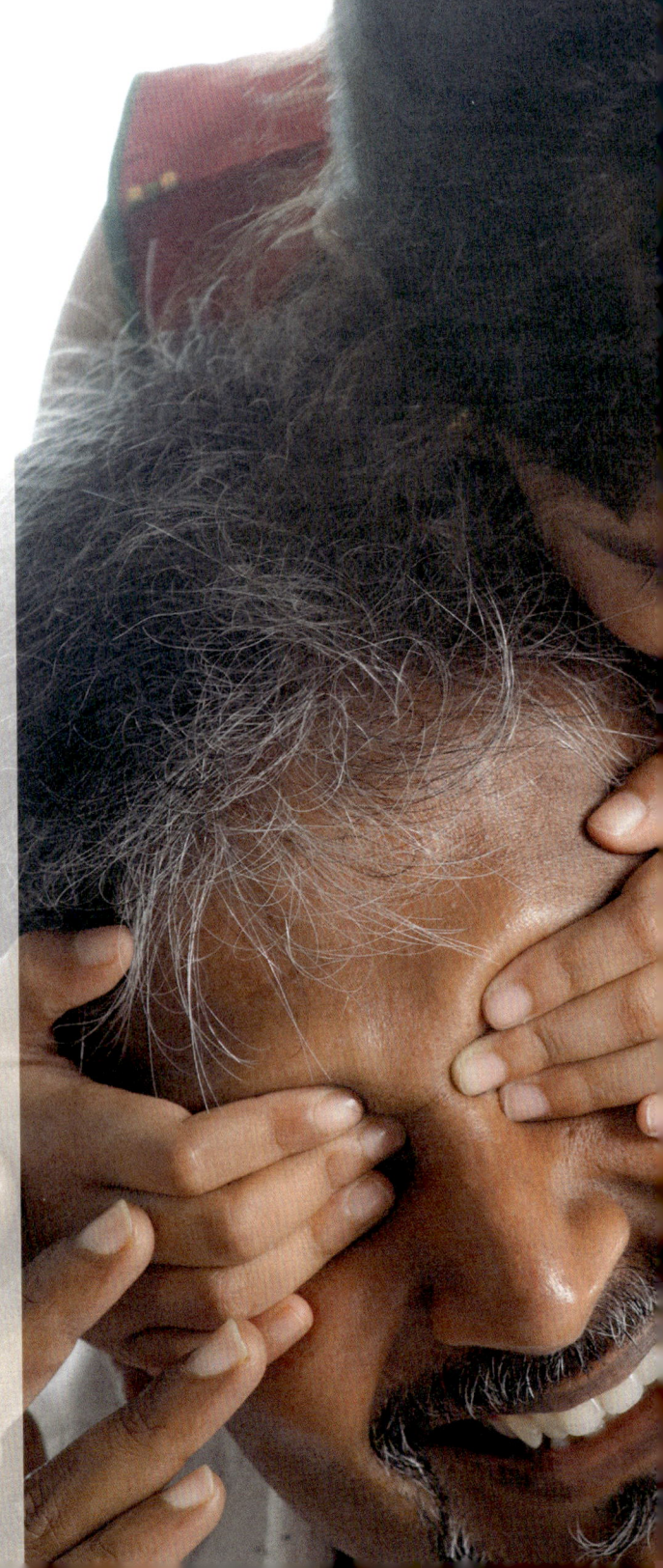

He has to be a guide, a compassionate disciplinarian, and a protector. He is usually the main source of income in the family. He shows his children unconditional love and support. Being a father is indeed a challenge.

Now, what does your dad deserve? Right: Your dad deserves a hug. Your hug speaks of your great love for him.

Aside from obligatory birthdays, Father's Day and Christmas celebrations, when are the times that you freely express your love for your dad through your powerful hugs?

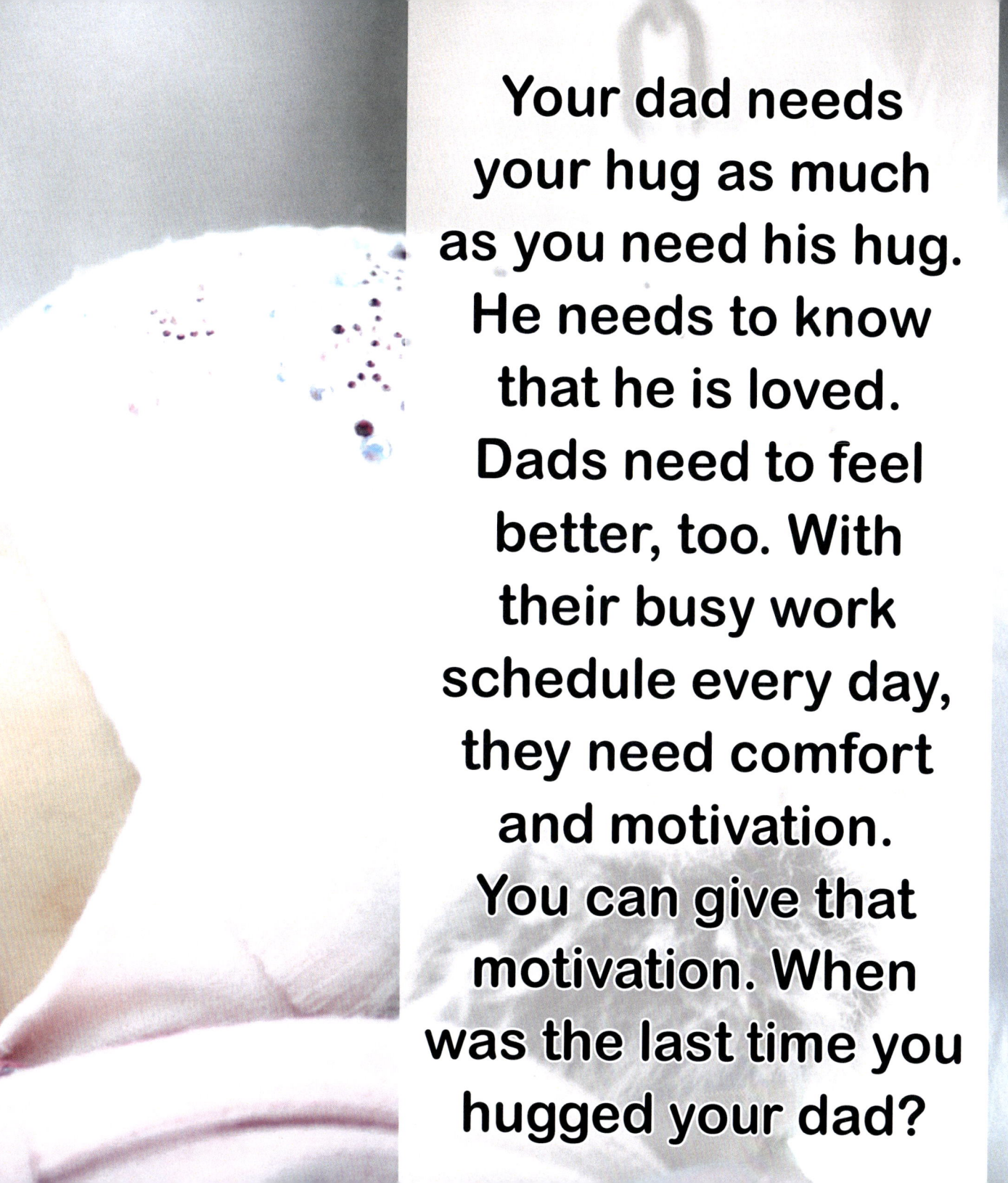

Your dad needs your hug as much as you need his hug. He needs to know that he is loved. Dads need to feel better, too. With their busy work schedule every day, they need comfort and motivation. You can give that motivation. When was the last time you hugged your dad?

The Smashing Powers of a Hug

Hugs are incredible expressions of love and care. They can make both people feel better. As you grow up, you find it hard sometimes to get along with your parents because you want to be independent. You want to do things for yourself. By just hugging any of them, you can show you still love and respect them.

Hugs strengthen the parent-child relationship. Share a hug. Make it real. Melting into each other's arms can ease pain and can bring comfort.

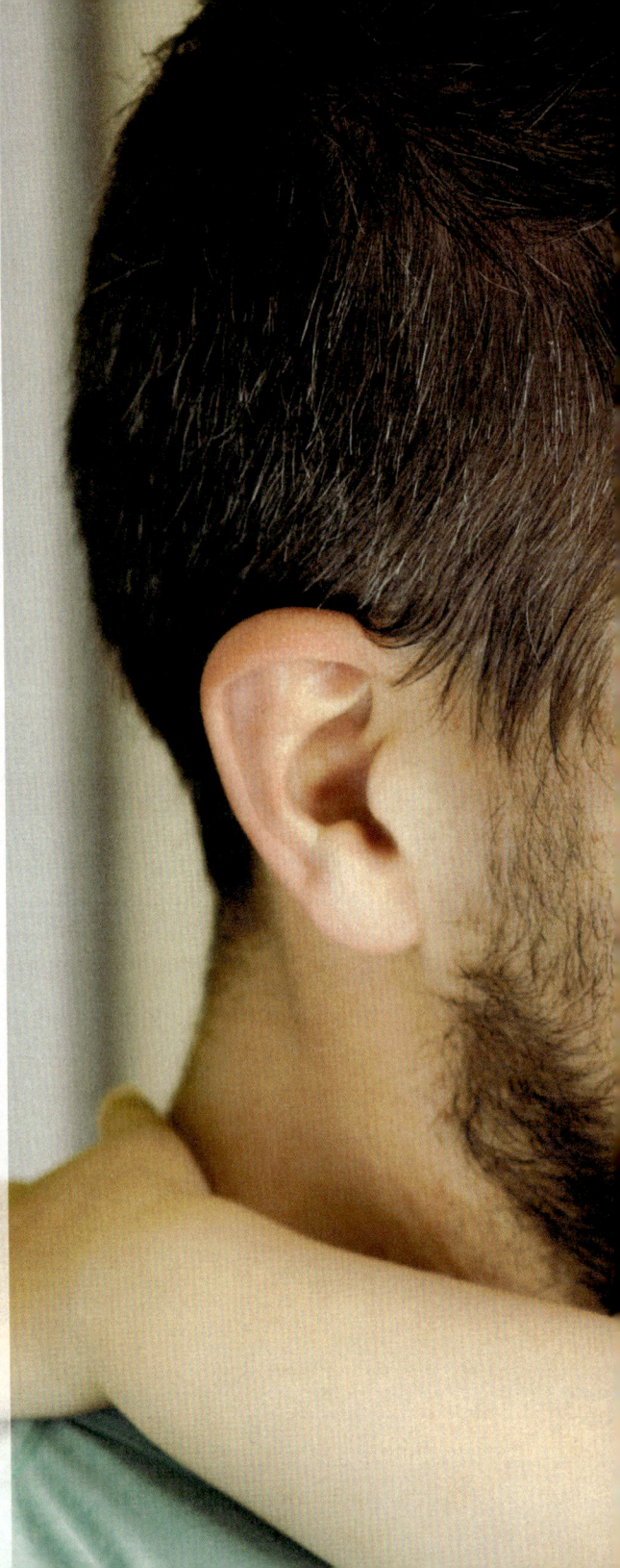

Hugging your dad makes him feel that he is important. He feels your unconditional love. He feels your respect.

A hug is a deep representation of trust. Whatever is out there, let your daddy feel that you trust him. Likewise, he will feel that his hard work as head of the family is well appreciated.

Hugging your dad is a creative way of telling him that you love him and deeply trust his efforts.

Hugs can wipe away grudges. A powerful hug that you give your dad will ease pain away. It makes him feel that you look up to him as your dad. He can sense your being thoughtful with your tight hugs.

Hugging your dad each and every day makes him feel special. It's a gesture that is worth more than anything money can buy.

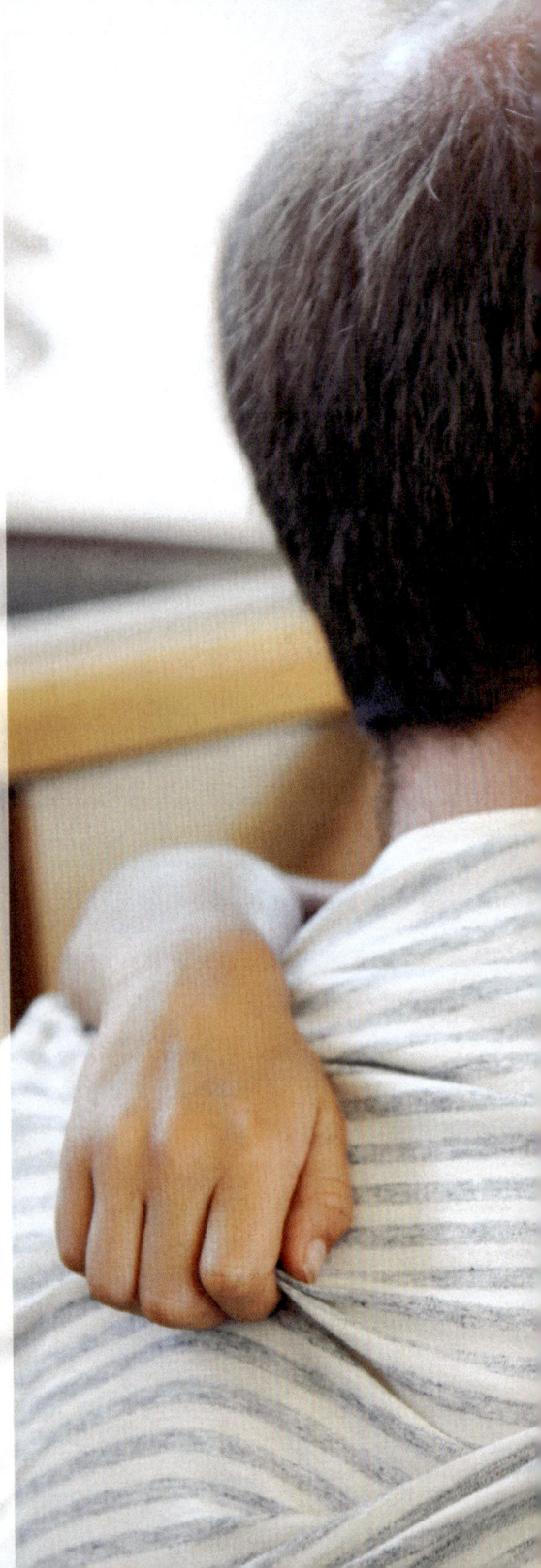

Even when it's not Father's Day, express to your dad your deepest appreciation for the efforts he extends for the family. Hugging him will tell him how much he means to you and how much he is appreciated. Remove his worries and ease his tedious days.

Now, do yourself a favor. Give your dad that inspiration. Hug your dad and mean it. Your dad loves your hugs. It means that you care for him.

It's a powerful gesture of love that can't be bought from any shop. It's free and its meaning is very deep.

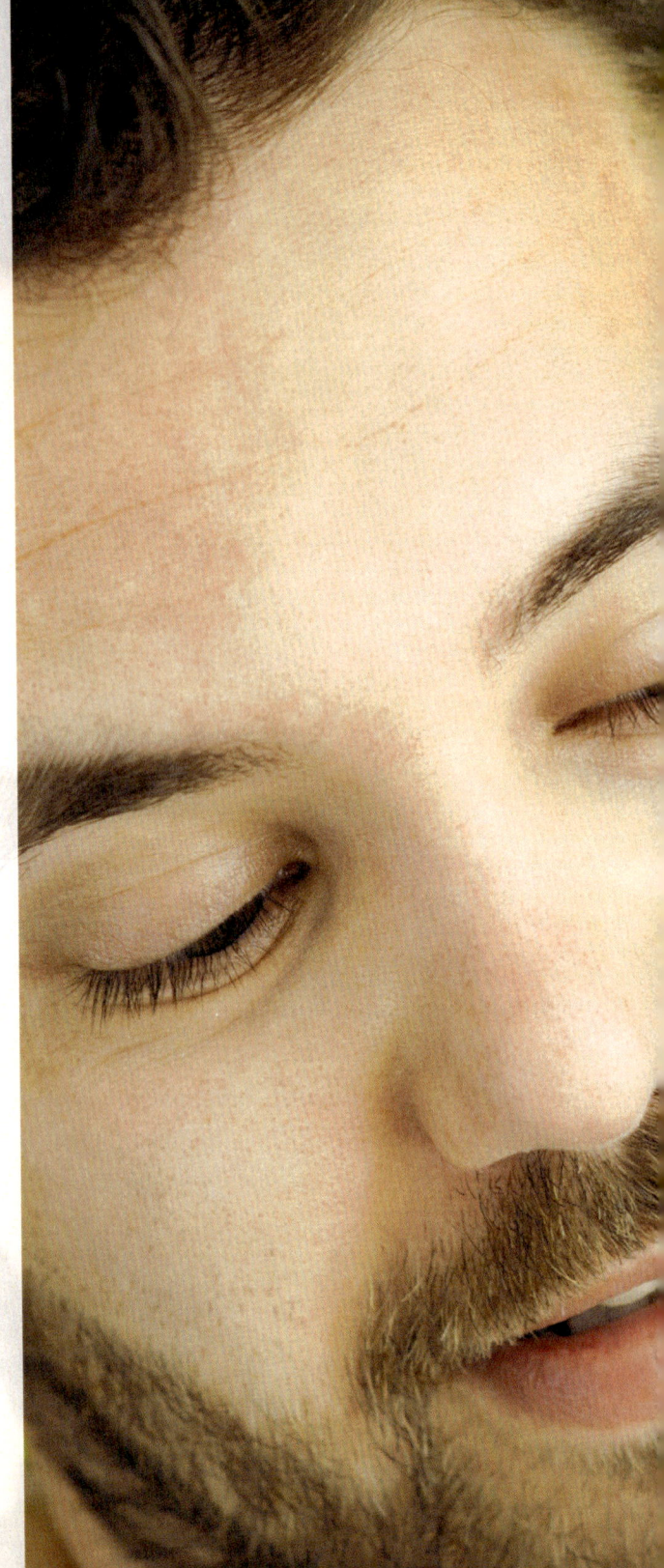

Made in the USA
Middletown, DE
01 June 2017